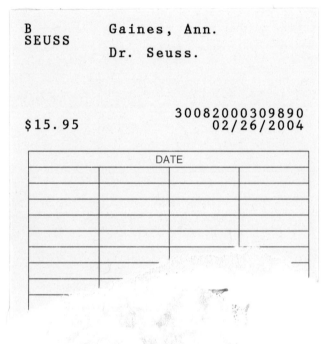

B
SEUSS

Gaines, Ann.

Dr. Seuss.

$15.95

30082000309890
02/26/2004

DATE			

DR. SEUSS

A Real-Life Reader Biography

Ann Graham Gaines

Mitchell Lane Publishers, Inc.
P.O. Box 619
Bear, Delaware 19701
www.mitchelllane.com

Printing   3   4   5   6   7   8   9   10

Real-Life Reader Biographies

Paula Abdul	Christina Aguilera	Marc Anthony	Lance Armstrong
Drew Barrymore	Tony Blair	Brandy	Garth Brooks
Kobe Bryant	Sandra Bullock	Mariah Carey	Aaron Carter
Cesar Chavez	Roberto Clemente	Christopher Paul Curtis	Roald Dahl
Oscar De La Hoya	Trent Dimas	Celine Dion	Sheila E.
Gloria Estefan	Mary Joe Fernandez	Michael J. Fox	Andres Galarraga
Sarah Michelle Gellar	Jeff Gordon	Virginia Hamilton	Mia Hamm
Melissa Joan Hart	Salma Hayek	Jennifer Love Hewitt	Faith Hill
Hollywood Hogan	Katie Holmes	Enrique Iglesias	Allen Iverson
Janet Jackson	Derek Jeter	Steve Jobs	Michelle Kwan
Bruce Lee	Jennifer Lopez	Cheech Marin	Ricky Martin
Mark McGwire	Alyssa Milano	Mandy Moore	Chuck Norris
Tommy Nuñez	Rosie O'Donnell	Mary Kate and Ashley Olsen	Rafael Palmeiro
Gary Paulsen	Colin Powell	Freddie Prinze, Jr.	Condoleezza Rice
Julia Roberts	Robert Rodriguez	J.K. Rowling	Keri Russell
Winona Ryder	Cristina Saralegui	Charles Schulz	Arnold Schwarzenegger
Selena	Maurice Sendak	**Dr. Seuss**	Shakira
Alicia Silverstone	Jessica Simpson	Sinbad	Jimmy Smits
Sammy Sosa	Britney Spears	Julia Stiles	Ben Stiller
Sheryl Swoopes	Shania Twain	Liv Tyler	Robin Williams
Vanessa Williams	Venus Williams	Tiger Woods	

Library of Congress Cataloging-in-Publication Data
Gaines, Ann.
     Dr. Seuss / Ann Graham Gaines.
         p. cm. — (A real-life reader biography)
     Includes index.
     ISBN 1-58415-074-2
     1. Seuss, Dr. — Juvenile literature. 2. Authors, American—20th century—Biography—Juvenile literature. 3. Illustrators—United States—Biography—Juvenile literature. 4. Children's literature—Authorship—Juvenile literature. [1. Seuss, Dr. 2. Authors, American. 3. Illustrators.] I. Title. II. Series.
PS3513.E2 Z68 2001
813'.52—dc21
     [B]
                                                                        00-067804

ABOUT THE AUTHOR: Ann Gaines holds graduate degrees in American Civilization and Library and Information Science from the University of Texas at Austin. She has been a freelance writer for 18 years, specializing in nonfiction for children. She lives near Gonzales, Texas with her husband and their four children.

PHOTO CREDITS: cover: Corbis; p. 4 Corbis; p. 7 Archive Photos; p. 16 Archive Photos; p. 28 Archive Photos; p. 29 Corbis

ACKNOWLEDGMENTS: The following story has been thoroughly researched, and to the best of our knowledge, represents a true story. While every possible effort has been made to ensure accuracy, the publisher will not assume liability for damages caused by inaccuracies in the data, and makes no warranty on the accuracy of the information contained herein.

Table of Contents

4

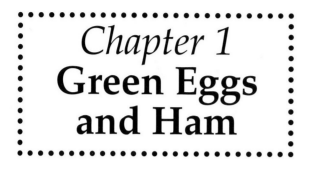

Chapter 1
Green Eggs and Ham

By 1960, author Dr. Seuss had already written many popular children's books for Random House Publishers. One day, for fun, the head of Random House, a man named Bennett Cerf, made a bet. He wagered Seuss $50 he could not produce a new book that used only 50 different words.

Seuss always enjoyed a challenge. And he possessed a great imagination. He loved to write and illustrate books for kids. He especially liked to write books that children who were just learning to read could enjoy.

Bennett Cerf bet Dr. Seuss that he could not make a book with just 50 words.

He had already achieved great success doing that. Kids had loved his first easy-to-read book, *The Cat in the Hat*. But that story contained more than 200 different words. Could he really write a book that used just a few words?

Back in his office, Seuss wrote down some ideas on a piece of paper and made a few sketches. Soon he created Sam-I-Am, a friendly, furry little creature. Then he came up with another character, this one a big, grumpy fellow. And finally he invented a wacky new kind of food. He had it!

His book would tell the story of Sam-I-Am and his efforts to get the stick-in-the-mud to try a new food, green eggs and ham. Over and over again, Sam-I-Am would offer it: in a house, with a mouse, in a box, with a fox, in the rain, on a train.

It took a long time, but Seuss finally felt satisfied and turned in the book to Bennett Cerf. Seuss had succeeded yet again, using small, easy words to write a funny story that

Seuss created *Green Eggs and Ham* using just 50 words!

grabbed the imagination of readers, taking them into a wild new world.

When *Green Eggs and Ham* was published, its cover proudly proclaimed "A 50-Word Book." Readers never felt cheated because of its lack of words. In fact, it would become one of Seuss's most popular books.

Here's proof of how many people read and remembered it. In 1985,

This photo taken in 1957, shows author/illustrator Dr. Seuss at his home office with a copy of his book, "The Cat in the Hat."

Princeton, a famous university in New Jersey, decided to honor Dr. Seuss by giving him an honorary degree. He expected to receive his diploma at a solemn ceremony.

Instead, he received a big surprise. When his name was announced, Seuss got up from his chair on the stage and started to walk toward the speakers' platform. Suddenly, the entire audience rose to its feet. It was filled with scientists and scholars who spent their days working in libraries and laboratories, people who were serious and studious. But not today! They all stood and recited Seuss's own silly words: "That Sam-I-Am, That Sam-I-Am, I do not like that Sam-I-Am. I do not like Green Eggs and Ham."

These were words these professors and students had first read 15, 20, 25 or even more years earlier. And they still knew them by heart.

This was the special gift Dr. Seuss possessed. He wrote and illustrated great books readers never forget.

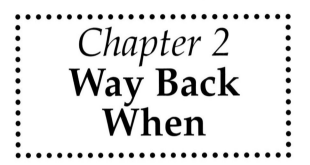

Chapter 2
Way Back When

Dr. Seuss is what is called a "pen name," the name under which an author writes. In real life, Dr. Seuss's name was Theodor Seuss Geisel. Geisel is pronounced GUY-zel.

Theodor Seuss Geisel was born on March 2, 1904, in the small city of Springfield, Massachusetts. His father, Theodor Robert Geisel, and mother, Henrietta Seuss Geisel, gave him his middle name in honor of his mother's family.

Theodor Seuss Geisel was an only child. Growing up, he felt close to both his parents. They were active people,

Dr. Seuss' real name is Theodor Geisel.

who enjoyed the outdoors and especially target shooting. They encouraged him in all he did. As a grown-up, he remembered his mother constantly praising him. She liked it when he used his imagination. He would later hold up his father as an example of a hard-working, well-liked man who earned people's respect.

At one time, Theodor's father managed a zoo.

The Geisel family owned a brewery (a factory which makes beer). It was one of the largest breweries in New England. But in 1920 it had to shut down because a new law called Prohibition made it illegal for Americans to drink alcoholic beverages. Mr. Geisel went to work for the city of Springfield. He managed the city's parks, including its great zoo. Like most women in those days, Henrietta Seuss Geisel was a homemaker.

The Geisels had a big, comfortable home in a nice neighborhood an easy walk from Forest Park. There was a monument in the park and Ted, as his parents called him, liked to climb its steep, winding stairs. That's why so many of the books he would write as a grown-up have the different characters going up and down lots of stairs.

He also loved to visit the zoo. "That zoo, that was where I learned whatever I know about animals," he later remembered.

When Geisel entered high school, he made many friends. He worked for his school newspaper, writing news articles and funny stories. He organized a music club and performed in school plays. His classmates voted him "Class Artist" and "Class Wit."

Theodor Geisel was never a very good student. His teachers always believed he did not perform to the best of his ability. But his grades were good enough for him to go to Dartmouth College. Once again he did not throw himself into his studies but devoted his time to making friends. His charm and wild sense of humor made him very popular.

Theodor loved to visit the zoo. That is where he learned so much about animals.

In college, Theodor called himself "Dr. Seuss," so his college dean wouldn't know who he was.

At Dartmouth, he was the editor-in-chief of the humor magazine, the *Jack-O-Lantern*. During his senior year, he got in trouble with the college dean, who ordered him to leave the magazine. But he continued to write for it, and that was when he began using his pen name of "Seuss" so that the dean wouldn't know who the author really was.

Chapter 3
Quick, Henry, the Flit!

Theodor Geisel graduated from college in 1925. His father had high hopes he would earn a doctorate degree and become a college professor. Wanting to make his father happy, the young man entered a competition for a scholarship to Oxford University, a very old and important school in England.

Before the winner was chosen, Ted told his father he had won. His father bragged to the Springfield newspaper. But Ted wasn't selected for the honor. His father was disappointed. But he felt that because he had already told the newspaper, he had to send Ted to

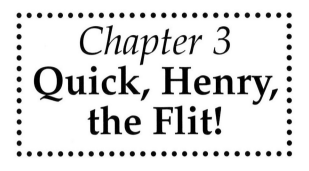

Theodor told his father he had won a scholarship to Oxford University, but he had not.

13

Oxford. So he gave his son the money to go to school there.

Theodor Seuss Geisel planned to earn a doctorate in English literature. But he was bored in his classes and realized he really was not suited to the life of a professor. What he really wanted was to become a cartoonist.

As a child, he had taken drawing lessons. One day, to get another view of his drawing, he turned it upside-down. The teacher scolded him, telling him a "real" artist would never do such a thing. He stopped going to the class. But he continued to draw.

"I was always drawing — with pencils, pens, crayons or anything. Nearly always, it was animals. Goofy-looking ones," he later said.

He constantly doodled in his school notebooks. Sometimes he drew what he saw, but more often he drew silly people and animals. At Oxford, another student watched him draw while everyone else took notes. She

> **Theodor planned to earn a doctorate in English literature. He found he liked drawing much better.**

commented, "You're not very interested in the lectures."

He admitted she was right. But he was very interested in her. Her name was Helen Palmer. They started to date.

They kept in touch even after Geisel dropped out of the university and started to travel around Europe. In places like London, Paris, and Rome, he made new friends who invited him to parties. Often he stayed up all night dancing the Charleston and drinking. But he also saw the sights. In Italy, he saw some of the world's greatest art. He spent days sitting in museums, with a sketchbook in his lap, copying famous paintings. Back in his hotel, he wrote many letters to Helen, describing all he saw and did.

At Oxford, Theodor met his wife-to-be, Helen Palmer.

In 1927, he returned to the United States. At first Geisel lived with his parents in Springfield. He told his father he planned one day to write a great novel. But in the meantime he hoped to earn his living as a cartoonist. He drew cartoons constantly which he sent off to newspapers and magazines. An editor at the famous *Life* magazine soon bought one for $25.

Within a few months, he felt confident he could succeed as a cartoonist and moved to New York City. There he landed a full-time job as a humor writer with a magazine named *Judge*.

Judge also published his cartoons. Once, for an issue that focused on the jungle, he drew a funny cover featuring animals. It looked a lot like his later illustrations for books — he had included an elephant with an extremely long trunk and a weird bird with a hooked beak and a long pink tail.

In November 1927, he and Helen were married in New York. They had a very

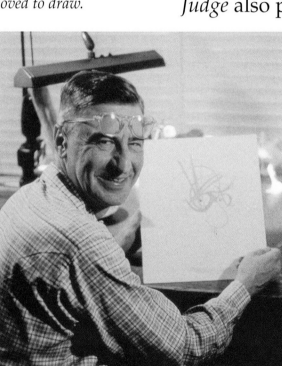

Dr. Seuss wanted to make a living as a cartoonist. He loved to draw.

happy life together. She encouraged him to experiment in his work, to try out the many new ideas that occurred to him. She also helped him meet deadlines and stay organized.

Thanks to Helen, Theodor Geisel was able not only to work for *Judge*, but also take on free-lance work. By now he was signing almost all his cartoons as "Dr. Seuss," perhaps because he had told his father a few years earlier that he would one day have his doctorate degree.

In a caption for one of his *Judge* cartoons in the late 1920s, Geisel mentioned Flit, an insecticide that killed fleas and mosquitoes. Geisel's cartoon showed a knight in a castle, sighing at the sight of a dragon. He complained because he had just sprayed with Flit (which Geisel imagined would have been needed for larger pests back in the Middle Ages).

A woman who was married to one of the men in charge of Flit's advertising saw the cartoon and laughed and

Helen encouraged Theodor to try many new things in his work.

laughed. She talked her husband into hiring Geisel. Over the next 17 years, he produced many cartoons for the Flit company. They always showed someone being tormented by bugs and used the same caption: "Quick, Henry, the Flit!" That became a catch phrase people all over America knew.

The Flit company paid him very well. He created advertising for more big companies like Standard Oil, Ford, and NBC (then a radio network). He also continued to write and draw cartoons for many magazines and newspapers. He used many different names on his work, including not just Dr. Seuss but also Theodore Seuss 2nd and Dr. Theophrastus Seuss.

The Geisels' income permitted them to travel a great deal. They discovered they loved California. They also returned many times to Europe.

Geisel liked this lifestyle very much. But sometimes his work bored him. Once he made a drawing poking fun at people who worked in advertising. It showed a man carrying a briefcase, jumping hurdles in his office.

He hoped at one time to draw a comic strip. A first installment of the strip he called Hejji appeared in 1935 in the many newspapers then owned by William Randolph Hearst. It featured a small boy named Hejji who came by chance into a new land named Baako. There he discovered many amazing things, including turtles that ran, goats with two heads, and a flower that broadcast music. When he picked the flower, he was seized by guards who dragged him off to appear before The Mighty One.

The strip looked great, but Americans never got to find out what happened to Hejji next. Hearst decided his newspapers were spending too much money and ordered the last three people hired for them fired.

But it was just a small setback. By this time, Geisel had thought of something else he wanted to try. Twice he had been hired to illustrate books of

Once he created a comic strip.

children's funny sayings. He started to think then about writing his own children's book.

His first idea came to him when he was 32. He and Helen were on a cruise when a storm came up. He was trying to take his mind off the waves that pounded the ship. Sitting in the bar, he was listening to the ship's engines when he realized they created a rhythm.

Suddenly he came up with words to fit: "I saw it all happen on Mulberry Street." Mulberry was one of the streets in his hometown of Springfield. He had a refrain. But what was it that happened on Mulberry Street? He covered a piece of stationery with ideas. He started with something people used to see every day: a horse and wagon. But then he proceeded to list things no one will ever see: a wagon pulled by a flying cat, a flying cat pulling a Viking ship, a Viking ship sailing up a volcano.

As he worked, his ideas changed into a story involving a boy whose father had told him he needed to go out

When he was in his 30s, Seuss decided he should be a children's writer.

on a walk to see what he could see. Really, he had just stopped to watch a worm, a cat, everyday things. But back describing his walk, the boy built up his story. He described to his dad amazing sights like an elephant decked out in red and gold carrying a rajah. To illustrate his story, Geisel made big drawings, packed with detail.

Theodor and Helen Geisel both loved this, his first book. But children's book editors did not. They said it was too different from everything else on the market. Nevertheless, he remained determined. He sent it to a total of 28 publishers. Every single one turned it down.

But finally Seuss bumped into an old friend who had just started to work as an editor for Vanguard Books. He accepted *And To Think That I Saw It On Mulberry Street*. It appeared in 1937. Dr. Seuss was given as the author's name. Theodor Geisel had begun what would become a new career, writing children's books.

His first book was *And To Think That I Saw It On Mulberry Street*.

Chapter 4
War!

In 1939, World War II broke out when Germany invaded Poland. Italy and Japan entered the war on the side of Germany. The Allies — Great Britain, France, and the Soviet Union — fought against them. For a time, the United States stayed out of the war. But after Japan bombed Pearl Harbor, Hawaii, on December 7, 1941, America entered the war to fight with the Allies.

Geisel had thought the U.S. should enter the war for a long time. He had already started to draw political cartoons for newspapers. Rather than just telling a joke, these cartoons

In 1942, Theodor joined the U.S. Army Signal Corps during the war.

commented on current events. His political cartoons often made fun of Germany, Italy, and Japan, the United States' enemies.

In 1942, he joined the U.S. Army Signal Corps. To make use of his special talents, the Army sent him to the Special Services Division in Hollywood. There he illustrated publications and made movies for the Army. He won two Oscar awards for his wartime movies, *Hitler Lives* and *Design for Death*.

World War II ended in 1945 and Americans rejoiced. Geisel left the Army. He and Helen moved to La Jolla, California. There he wrote and illustrated children's books for a new publisher, Random House.

Over time, Geisel wrote close to 50 more books. Many of them included memorable characters. He created a loyal elephant named Horton and a big-hearted moose named Thidwick. Always he went far beyond reality. For *On Beyond Zebra* and *If I Ran the Circus* he invented ridiculous new animals that

The Army sent him to a Special Services Division in Hollywood. There he illustrated publications and made movies for the Army.

In 1957,
Theodor
published
*The Cat in
the Hat* to
help young
children
learn to
read.

could perform marvelous tricks. His early books were all quite long. They were written in verse and included big words, including some Seuss had made up.

But in 1957 he tried something new. Teachers in American elementary schools had been reporting more and more of their students were having trouble learning to read. In an article in *Life* magazine, a famous writer named John Hersey said he thought the problem was simple: schools were teaching kids to read using boring books. He gave *Fun with Dick and Jane* as an example. Dick and Jane were quiet and polite children who always kept clean. Their fun was always very tame.

Seuss set his mind to solving the problem Hersey had described — how to write a lively book for children who were still sounding out words. He sat down at his desk with a list of short words like cat, hat, and mat and set to work. A man with a vivid imagination who liked real-life children, children who got dirty and sometimes acted naughty, Seuss came up with *The Cat in the Hat*.

Everybody loved this story of the cat who arrived to cheer up children stuck inside on a rainy day. Children laughed over the funny story and the pictures that showed the giant mess the cat made. They asked for more of the same. *The Cat in the Hat* made Dr. Seuss famous.

In 1957, Bennett Cerf offered Theodor and Helen Geisel new jobs. Theodor Geisel became president of Random House's new Beginner Books division. Helen Palmer Geisel became its vice president. Some other Beginner Books were written by Geisel under his old pen name, Dr. Seuss, as well as a new one, Theo. LeSeig. He and Helen also helped other writers create great easy-to-read books.

The Cat in the Hat made Dr. Seuss famous.

Chapter 5
A National Treasure

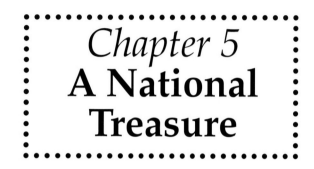

In 1967, his wife, Helen died.

In 1967, Helen Palmer Geisel died. The next year, Geisel married Audrey Stone Diamond. She also helped him with his writing.

As the years went by, he gained great fame as his books sold in greater and greater numbers. His work developed into spin-offs such as Dr. Seuss toys and television specials like *The Grinch Who Stole Christmas*.

Children continued to love his books and other work. Adults especially admired him, too, for his ability to convey a lesson in a funny way. His book *The Lorax* warned about the dangers of pollution. *The Butter Battle* told the story of how two nations became involved in a war by mistake, over a small matter.

Despite his fame, Theodor Geisel remained a private man who seldom made public appearances or granted interviews. But although he was not very interested in talking to grown-ups about his work, he felt great pleasure in hearing from children. Many would write and send him pictures over the years. He saved everything they sent.

On one occasion he did show a visitor around his studio. He talked about how much effort he put into every book. On his desk, he had a thick file of papers on which he had made notes of ideas or quick sketches. Some of his ideas would never make their way into a book. But he followed many others through to the end.

To make the book called *You're Only Old Once* he had made "working roughs," drawings on tracing paper in color. Then he wrote or typed up bits of

Despite his fame, Dr. Seuss remained a private man who rarely made public appear— ances or gave interviews.

text and pasted them onto his pictures. Later, when he was satisfied, he would make finished drawings in pen and ink. The publisher would make black and white prints of them, which he would then color in by hand. Later he would work on the cover. In the meantime, he would have fiddled with the text, too, getting it exactly right. As he told his visitor, "It takes more than an afternoon to write a book, hmmmmmmmmmm?"

Over time, he received many awards and honors. He won a Peabody award for *The Grinch who Stole Christmas* television special. Then he won the critics award at the International Animated Cartoon Festival for a cartoon based on *The Lorax*. In 1976, the

Dr. Seuss enjoyed reading his books to children. Here he is in 1957 reading to some children in La Jolla, California.

California Association of Teachers of English gave him its very first Outstanding California Author Award.

In 1980, the American Library Association gave him an award for service to children. Four years later, he received the Pulitzer Prize, the highest honor an American author can receive. And in 1986, the San Diego Museum of Art organized an exhibit that featured his artwork, including cartoons and illustrations from over 60 years.

Dr. Seuss lived to be 87 years old. He worked til the end. He left an unfinished manuscript on his desk when he died.

Years after his death, Dr. Seuss lives on, and his books remain as popular as ever with children all over.

On September 24, 1991, Theodor Geisel died at the age of 87. His death made headlines the world over. Many people remembered how he had enriched their lives by creating so many beloved books. To the end, he remained at work. On his desk he left sketches and an unfinished manuscript.

After his death, his books remained in print. Random House, with the aid of Audrey Geisel, continued to bring out new Dr. Seuss books, videos, and games based on his earlier works. His hometown of Springfield, Massachusetts erected a memorial to him. A movie version of *The Grinch Who Stole Christmas* starred the famous comic actor Jim Carrey and drew millions of people when it was released in 2000.

All over the world people continued to enjoy the life and works of this very special man. But with all the honors that came to Dr. Seuss, there was one thing that he never got. Random House Publisher Bennett Cerf never paid that $50 bet.

Selected Dr. Seuss Books

And to Think That I Saw It on Mulberry Street (New York: Vanguard Books, 1937; New York: Random House, 1989).

Bartholomew & the Oobleck (New York: Random House, 1949).

The Butter Battle Book (New York: Random House, 1984).

The Cat in the Hat (New York: Random House, 1957).

The Cat in the Hat Comes Back! (New York: Random House, 1958).

Daisy-Head Mayzie (New York: Random House, c1994).

The Five Hundred Hats of Bartholomew Cubbins (New York: Vanguard Press, c1938; New York: Random House, 1990).

Fox in Socks (New York: Random House, 1965).

Green Eggs and Ham (New York: Random House, 1960).

Happy Birthday to You (New York: Random House, 1959).

Hop on Pop (New York: Random House, 1963).

Horton Hatches the Egg (New York: Random House, 1940).

Horton Hears a Who (New York: Random House, 1954).

How the Grinch Stole Christmas (New York: Random House, 1957).

I Can Lick Thirty Tigers Today & Other Stories (New York: Random House, 1969).

I Had Trouble in Getting to Solla Sollew (New York: Random House, 1992).

If I Ran the Circus (New York: Random House, 1956).

If I Ran the Zoo (New York: Random House, 1950).

The Lorax (New York: Random House, [1971]).

McElligot's Pool (New York: Randon House, 1947).

Marvin K. Mooney, Will You Please Go Now? (New York: Random House, 1972).

On Beyond Zebra (New York: Random House 1955).

One Fish, Two Fish, Red Fish, Blue Fish (New York: Random House, 1960).

Sneetches & Other Stories (New York: Random House, 1969).

There's a Wocket in My Pocket! (New York: Random House, 1974).

Thidwick, the Big-Hearted Moose (New York: Random House, 1948).

Yertle the Turtle & Other Stories (New York: Random House, 1958).

You're Only Old Once! (New York: Random House, 1986).

Chronology

- 1904, born on March 2 in Springfield, Massachusetts.
- 1918, enters high school
- 1921, graduates from Springfield High School and enrolls at Dartmouth College.
- 1925, enrolls at Oxford University in England, hoping to earn a doctorate degree.
- 1926, drops out of Oxford and starts to travel all over Europe.
- 1927, returns to the United States where he works as a cartoonist; in November, marries Helen Palmer.
- 1935, is hired to create a comic strip, but then immediately fired (due to no fault of his own).
- 1937, publishes his first children's book, *To Think That I Saw It on Mulberry Street.*
- 1940, starts to draw editorial cartoons.
- 1942, joins the Army, which assigns him to the Signal Corps.
- 1946, moves to California; by now Random House is publishing Dr. Seuss's books.
- 1957, begins to write a new sort of children's book for beginning readers.
- 1958, begins working for Random House along with his wife, heading up its new Beginner Books division.
- 1967, Helen Palmer Geisel dies.
- 1968, marries his second wife, Audrey.
- 1971, wins a Peabody award for television special *The Grinch Who Stole Christmas.*
- 1984, receives the Pulitzer Prize.
- 1991, dies on September 24 at the age of 87.
- 2000, movie version of *The Grinch Who Stole Christmas* is released.

Index